IT'S TIME TO EAT RED RICE AND SAUSAGE

It's Time to Eat RED RICE AND SAUSAGE

Walter the Educator

Silent King Books
A WhichHead Entertainment Imprint

Copyright © 2024 by Walter the Educator

All rights reserved. No part of this book may be reproduced in any manner whatsoever without written per- mission except in the case of brief quotations embodied in critical articles and reviews.

First Printing, 2024

Disclaimer

This book is a literary work; the story is not about specific persons, locations, situations, and/or circumstances unless mentioned in a historical context. Any resemblance to real persons, locations, situations, and/or circumstances is coincidental. This book is for entertainment and informational purposes only. The author and publisher offer this information without warranties expressed or implied. No matter the grounds, neither the author nor the publisher will be accountable for any losses, injuries, or other damages caused by the reader's use of this book. The use of this book acknowledges an understanding and acceptance of this disclaimer.

It's Time to Eat RED RICE AND SAUSAGE is a collectible early learning book by Walter the Educator suitable for all ages belonging to Walter the Educator's Time to Eat Book Series. Collect more books at WaltertheEducator.com

USE THE EXTRA SPACE TO TAKE NOTES AND DOCUMENT YOUR MEMORIES

RED RICE AND SAUSAGE

It's time to eat, come take a seat,

It's Time to Eat
Red Rice and Sausage

A yummy dish that's such a treat.

Red rice and sausage, piping hot,

A meal we'll love, it hits the spot!

The rice is red, the sausage shines,

A mix of flavors so divine.

Tomatoes, spices, cooked just right,

A dinner full of pure delight.

The sausage sizzles, juicy and round,

Its tasty smell will surely astound.

The rice is fluffy, seasoned so well,

Its savory magic, you can tell.

With every bite, a hearty cheer,

For food that brings us all so near.

Around the table, smiles abound,

As laughter and joy spread all around.

It's Time to Eat
Red Rice
and
Sausage

We thank the cook, so full of pride,

For this delicious dish supplied.

Each spoonful's warmth is a hug so sweet,

Red rice and sausage, what a treat!

Let's count the sausages, one, two, three,

Sharing with friends and family.

The rice is plenty, we'll have our fill,

The perfect dinner to make us still.

A dash of spice, a touch of love,

This meal's a gift from up above.

Each bite is bold, each taste is new,

Oh, red rice and sausage, we love you!

So grab your fork and take a bite,

This dish will make your heart feel light.

A meal to share, to laugh and play,

It's Time to Eat
Red Rice
and
Sausage

It turns an evening into a day.

When dinner's done, we'll clean our plate,

And thank the stars for food so great.

Red rice and sausage, always the best,

It's the dish that passes every test!

Now let's all cheer, a great hooray,

For red rice and sausage saves the day.

It fills us up and makes us smile,

It's Time to Eat Red Rice and Sausage

A meal worth waiting for a while!

ABOUT THE CREATOR

Walter the Educator is one of the pseudonyms for Walter Anderson. Formally educated in Chemistry, Business, and Education, he is an educator, an author, a diverse entrepreneur, and he is the son of a disabled war veteran. "Walter the Educator" shares his time between educating and creating. He holds interests and owns several creative projects that entertain, enlighten, enhance, and educate, hoping to inspire and motivate you. Follow, find new works, and stay up to date with Walter the Educator™

at WaltertheEducator.com

www.ingramcontent.com/pod-product-compliance
Lightning Source LLC
LaVergne TN
LVHW052014060526
838201LV00059B/4032